DARK WHIMSY

Adult Coloring Book

BY DIANA GRAVES

www.dianagraves.org

DEDICATION

My daughter Morrighan Raven Graves

(MO, MOGY, MOZY, MORGAN FREEMAN)

Your mom will always love you!

.

CONTENTS

ACKNOWLEDGMENTS

IPPICY.COM
&
CONVERT.TOWN.COM

The artwork you are about to enjoy are all hand drawn musings. I was later told that how I draw is something called…Zantange. I had no idea what I did was a thing. You would think I don't hang out online enough or something.

I did this mostly with a computer after being told my thing was an actual thing people did with computer programs…

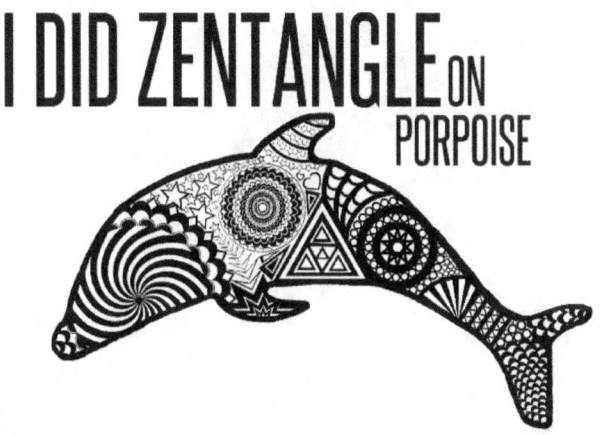

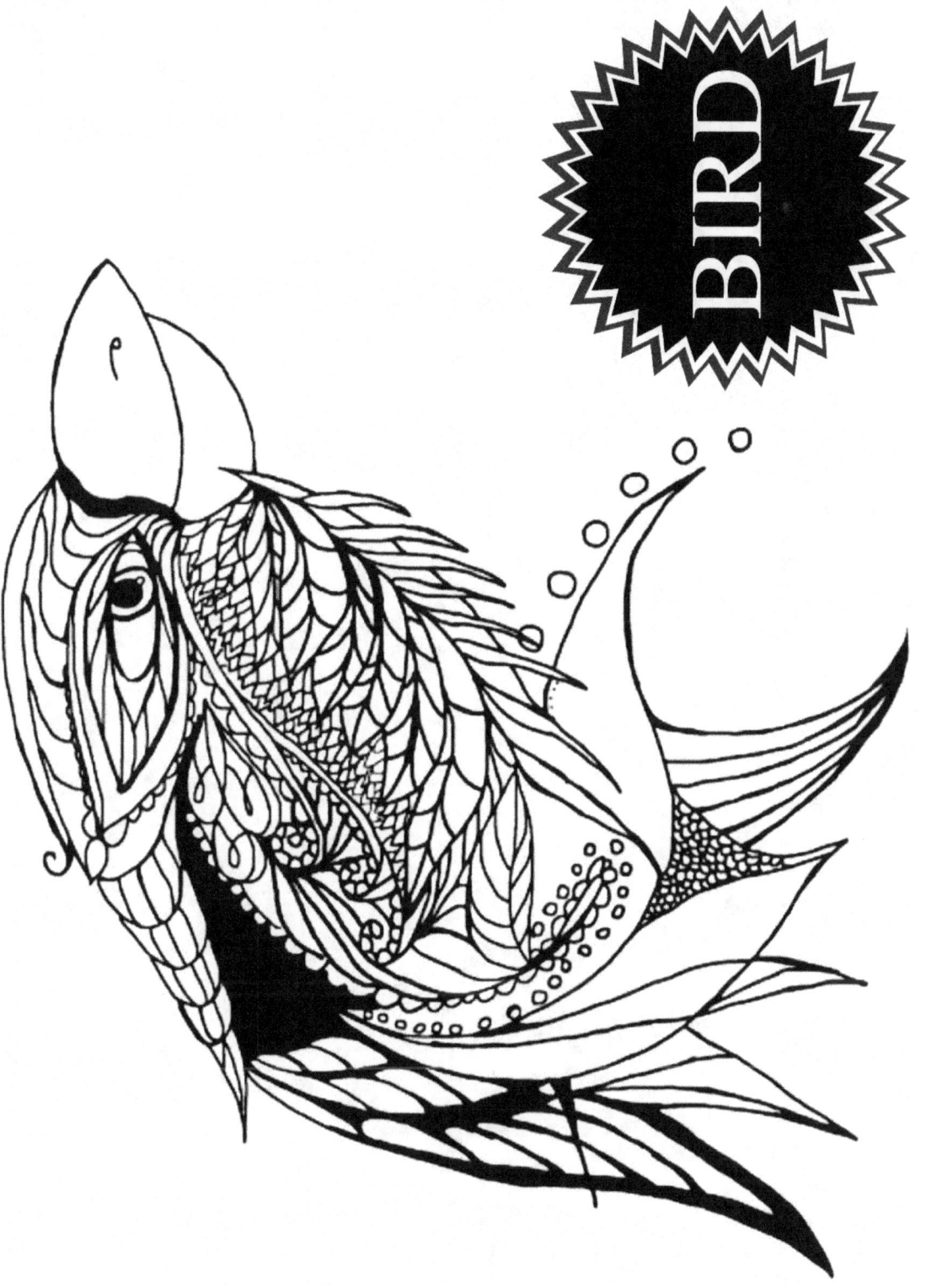

BIRD

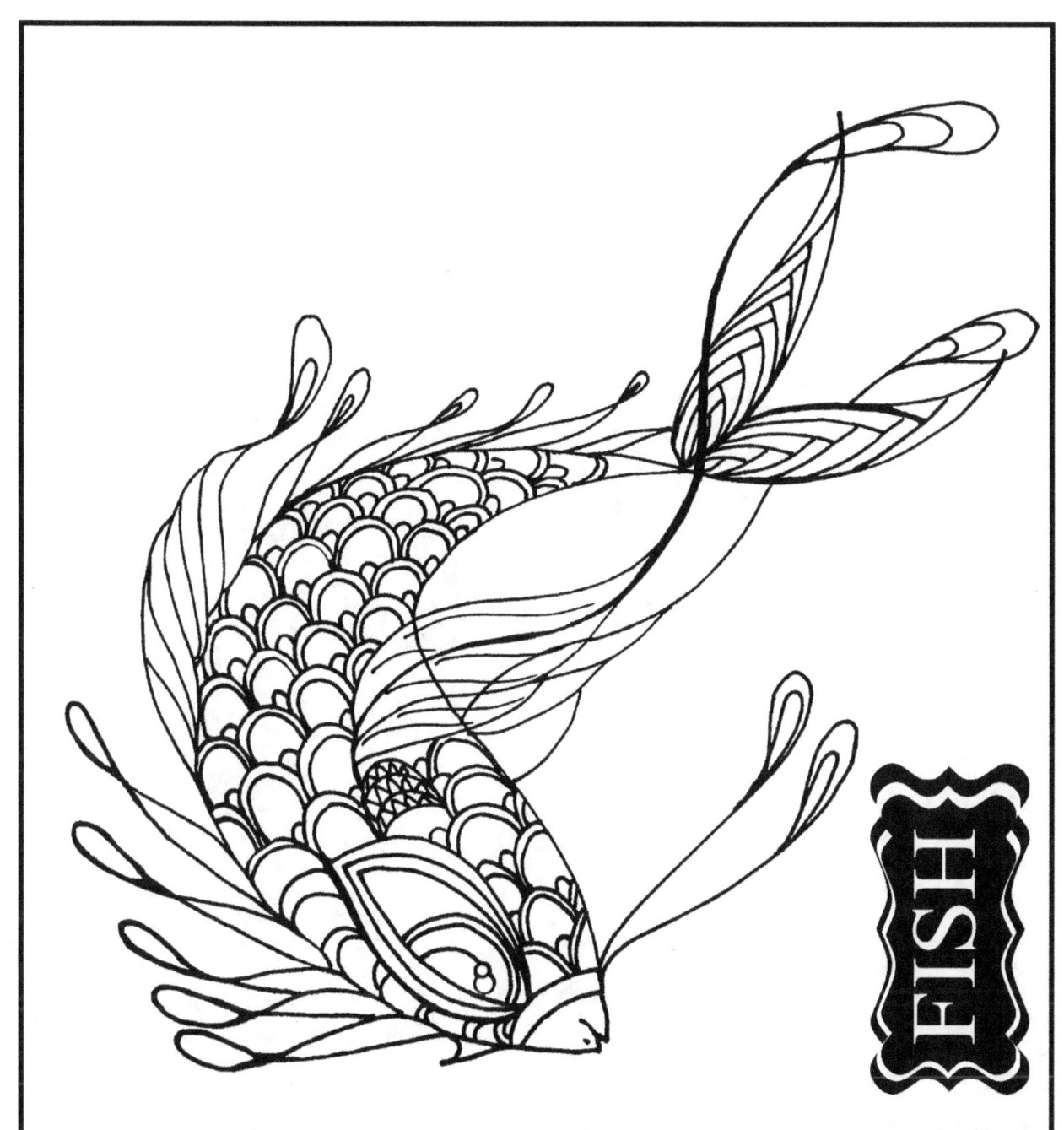

FISH

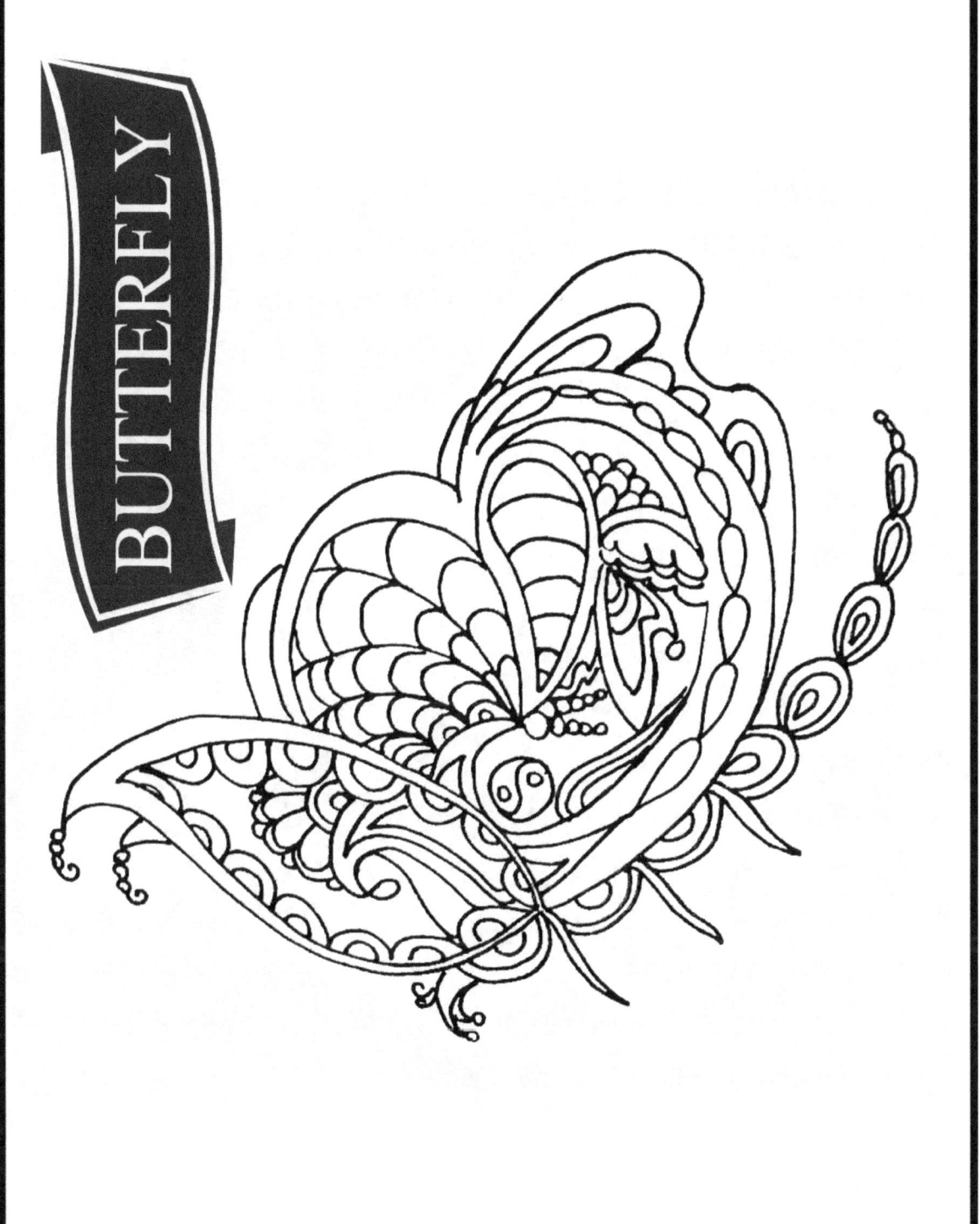

BUTTERFLY

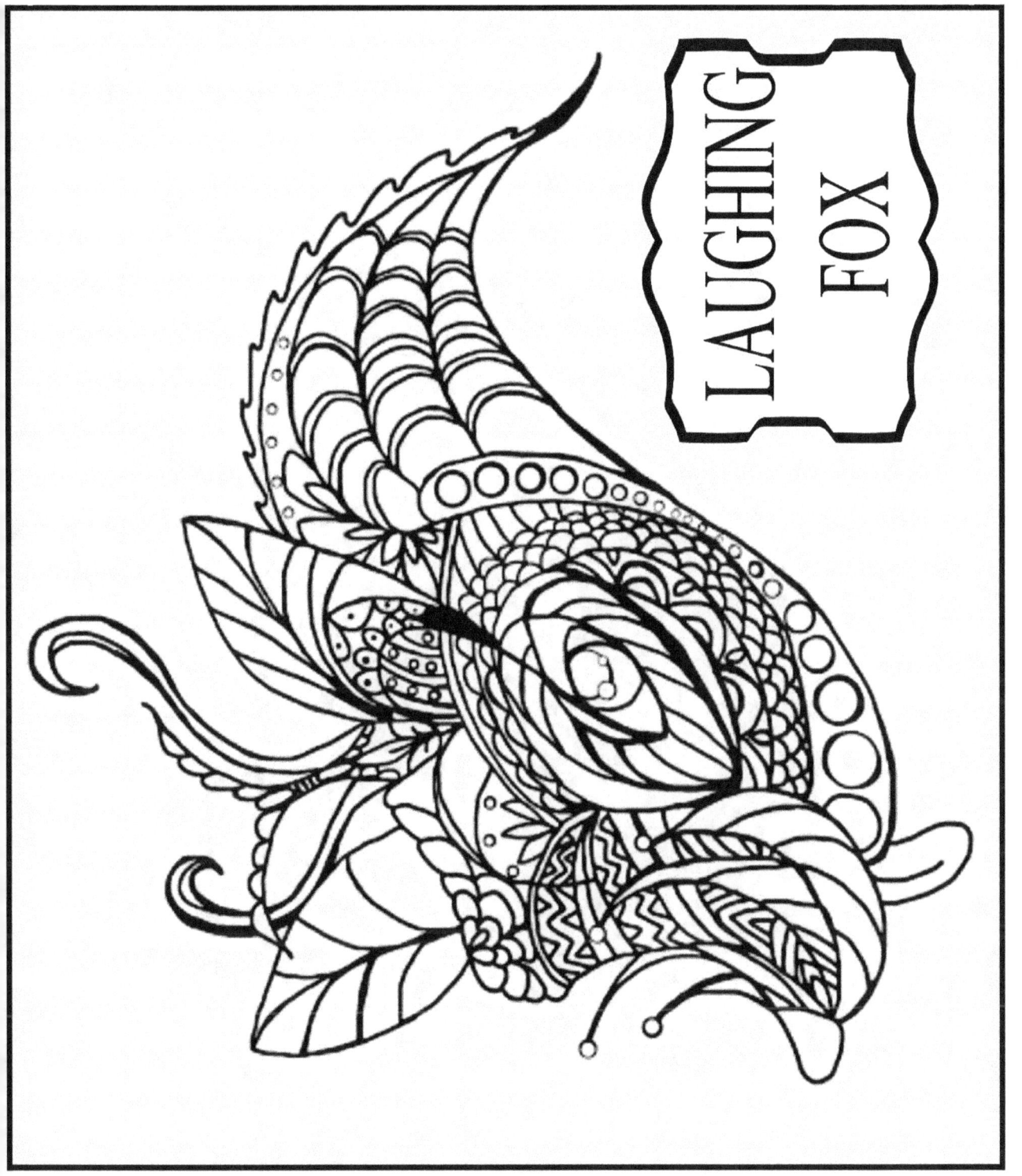

LAUGHING FOX

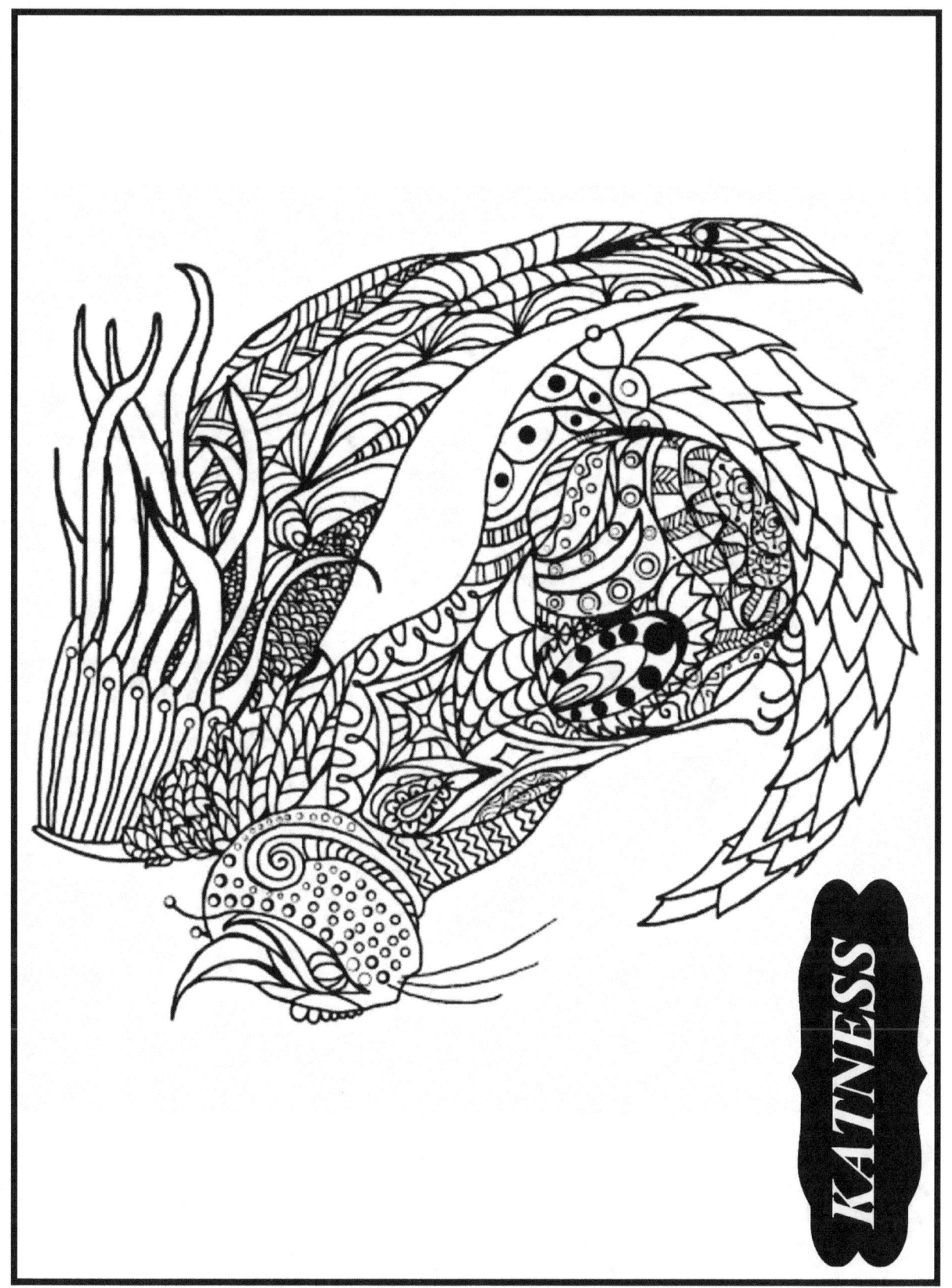

KATNESS

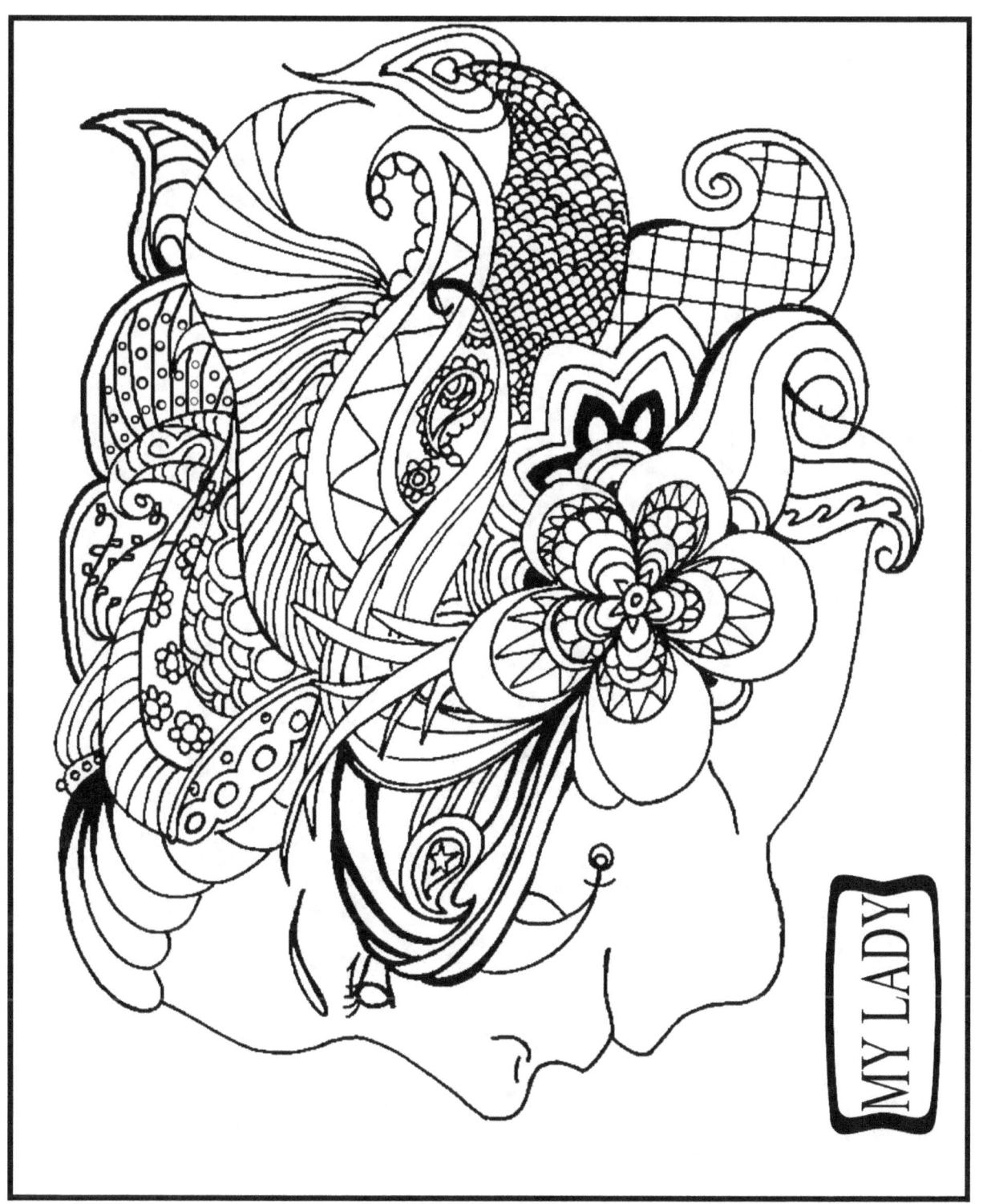

MY LADY

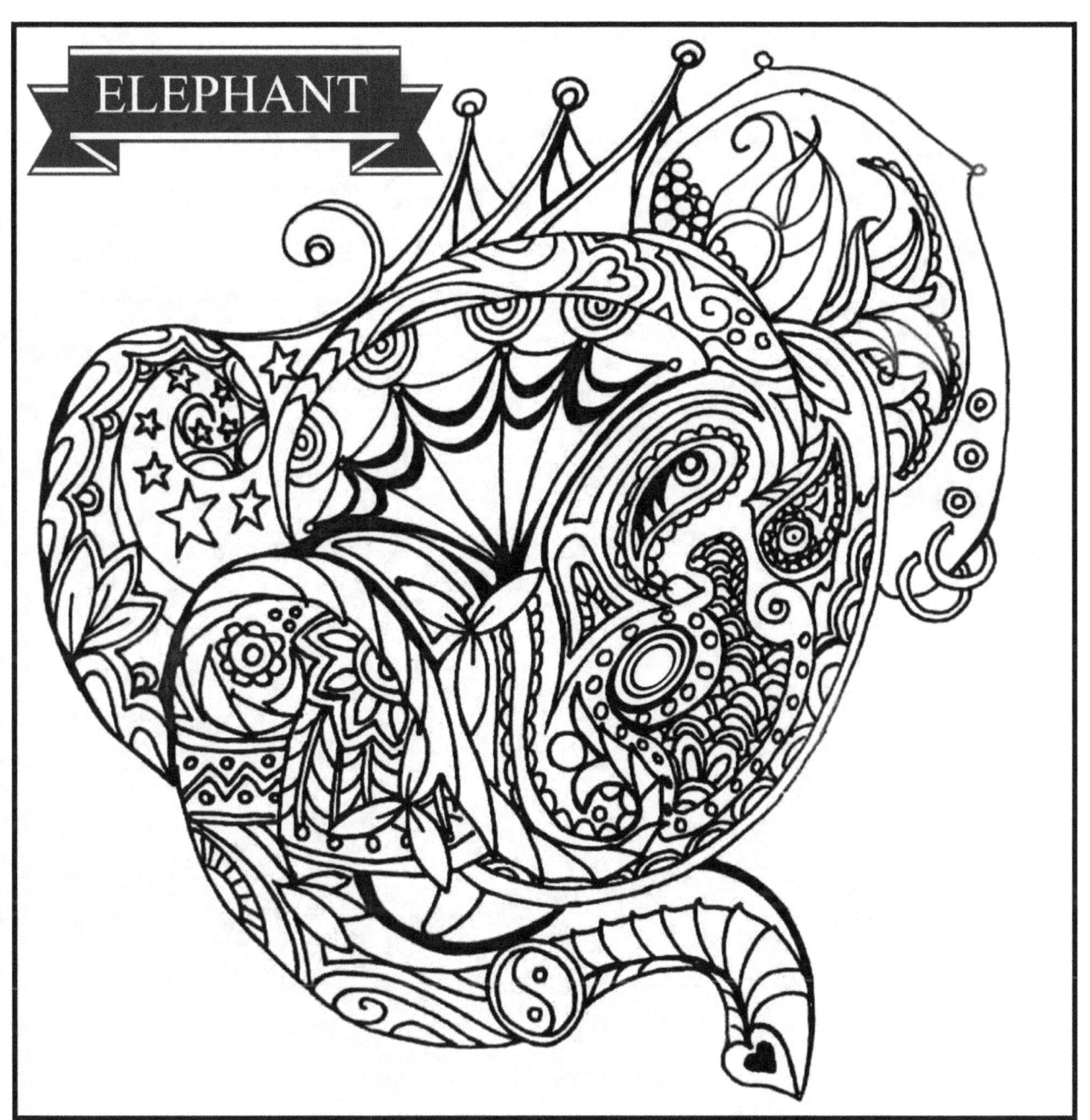

ELEPHANT

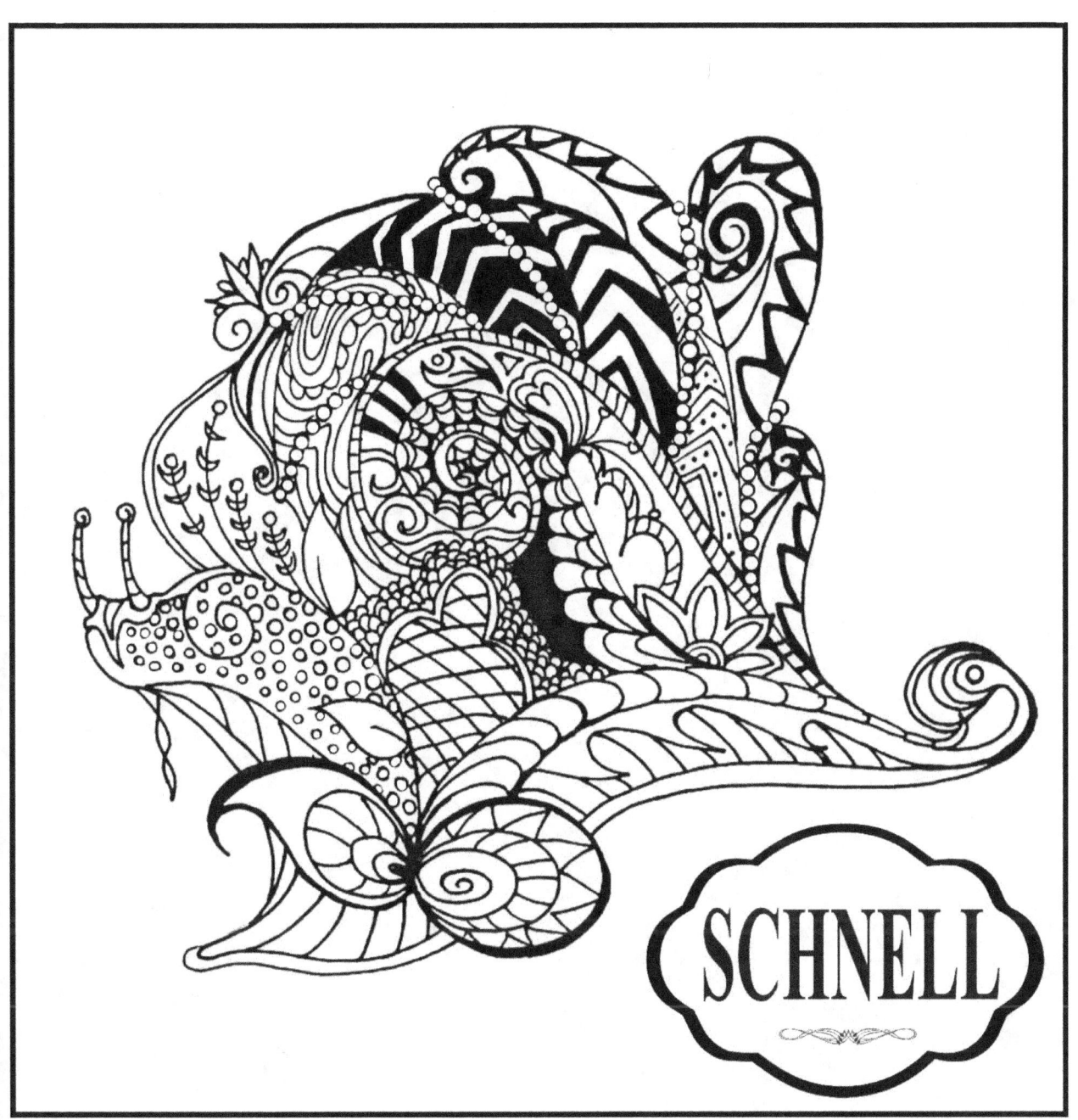

SCHNELL

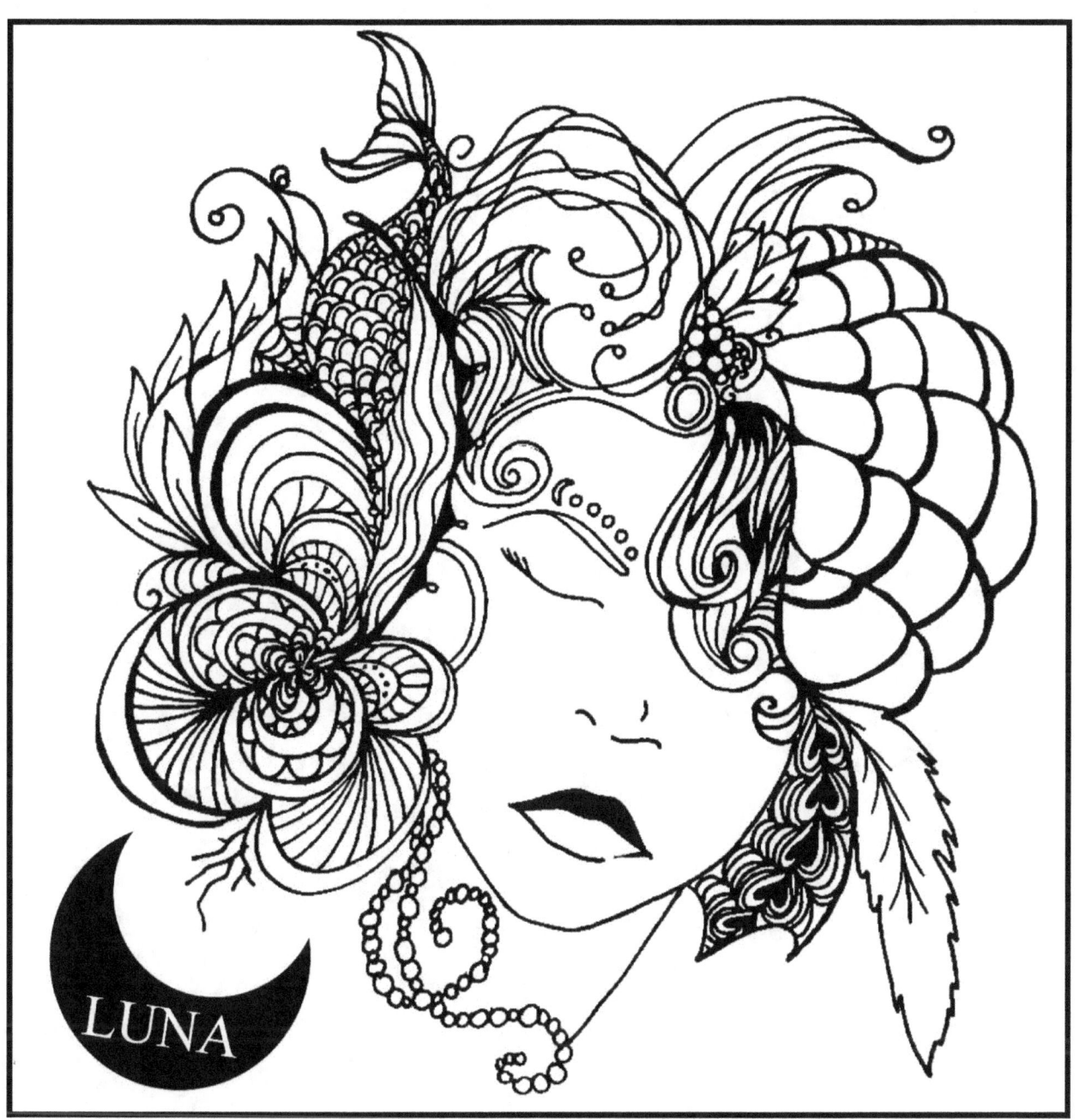

LUNA

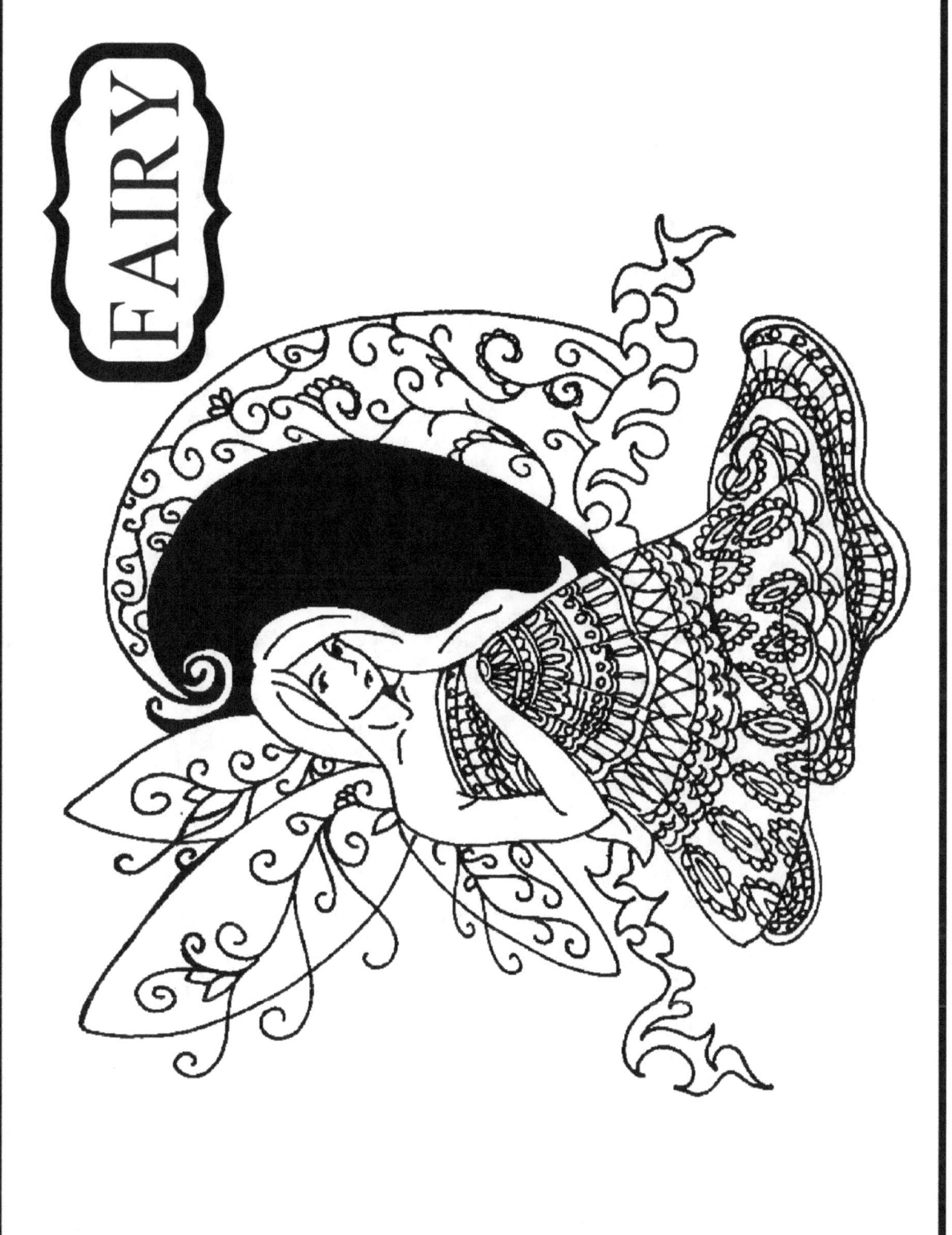

FAIRY

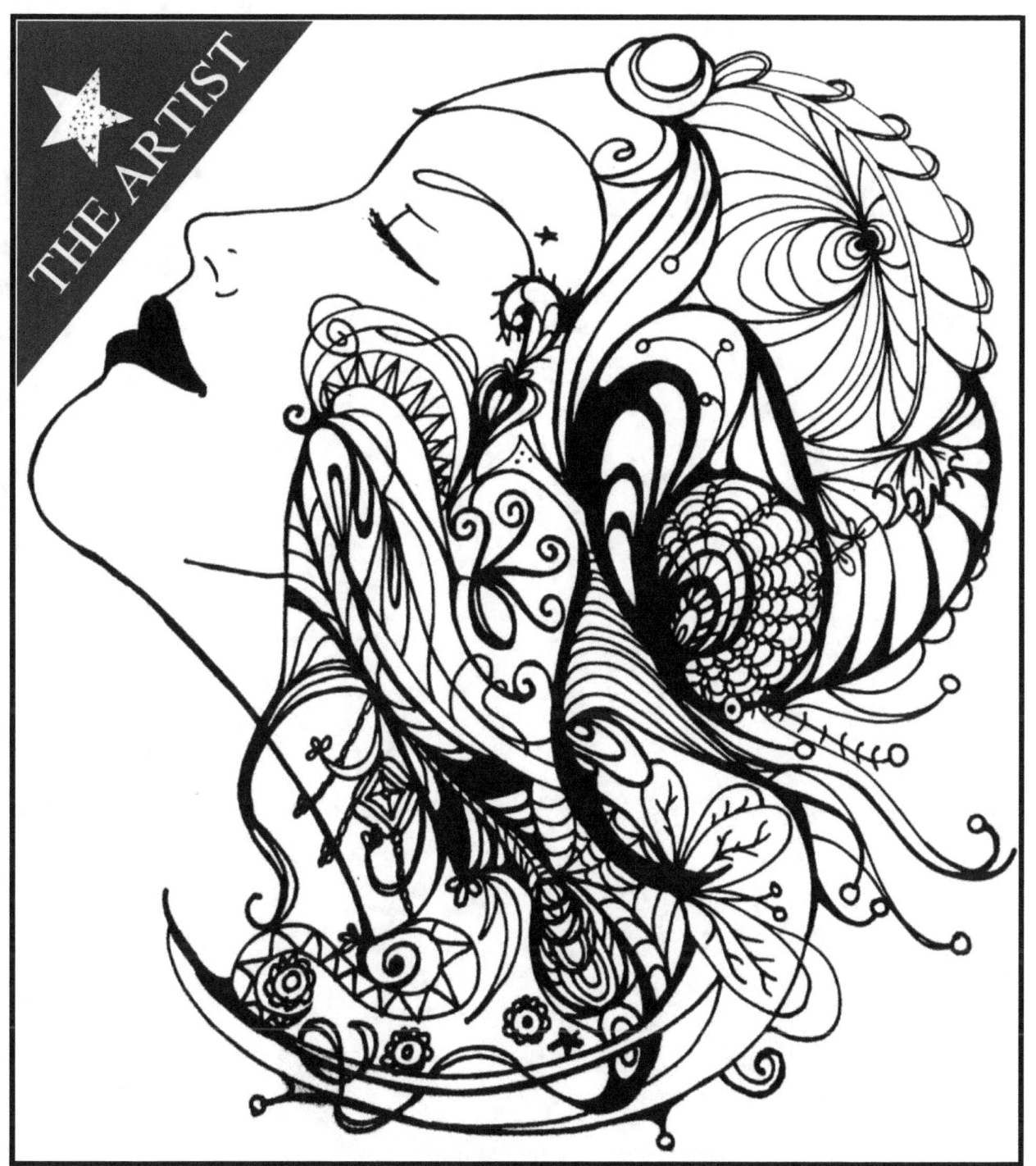

21

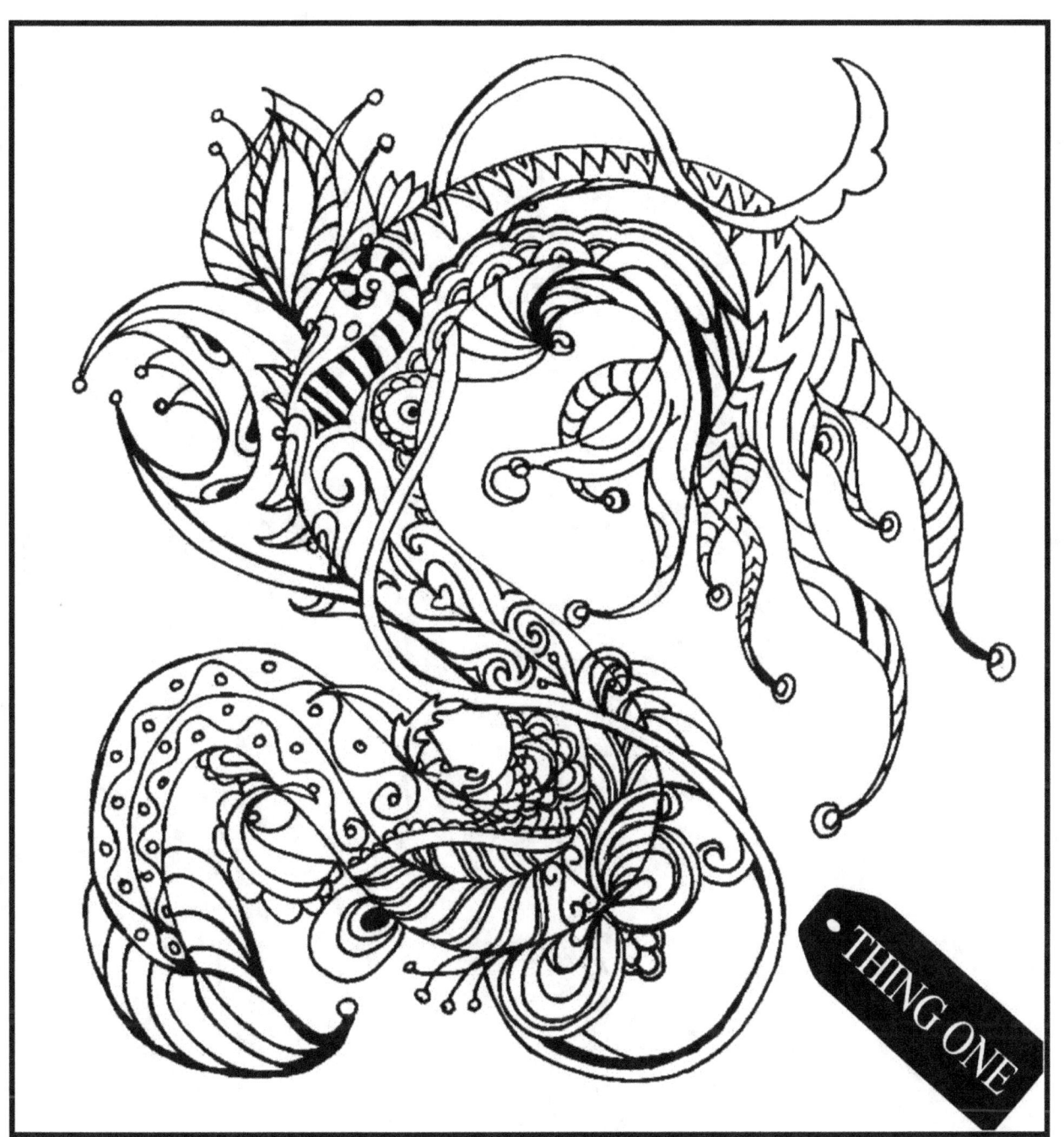

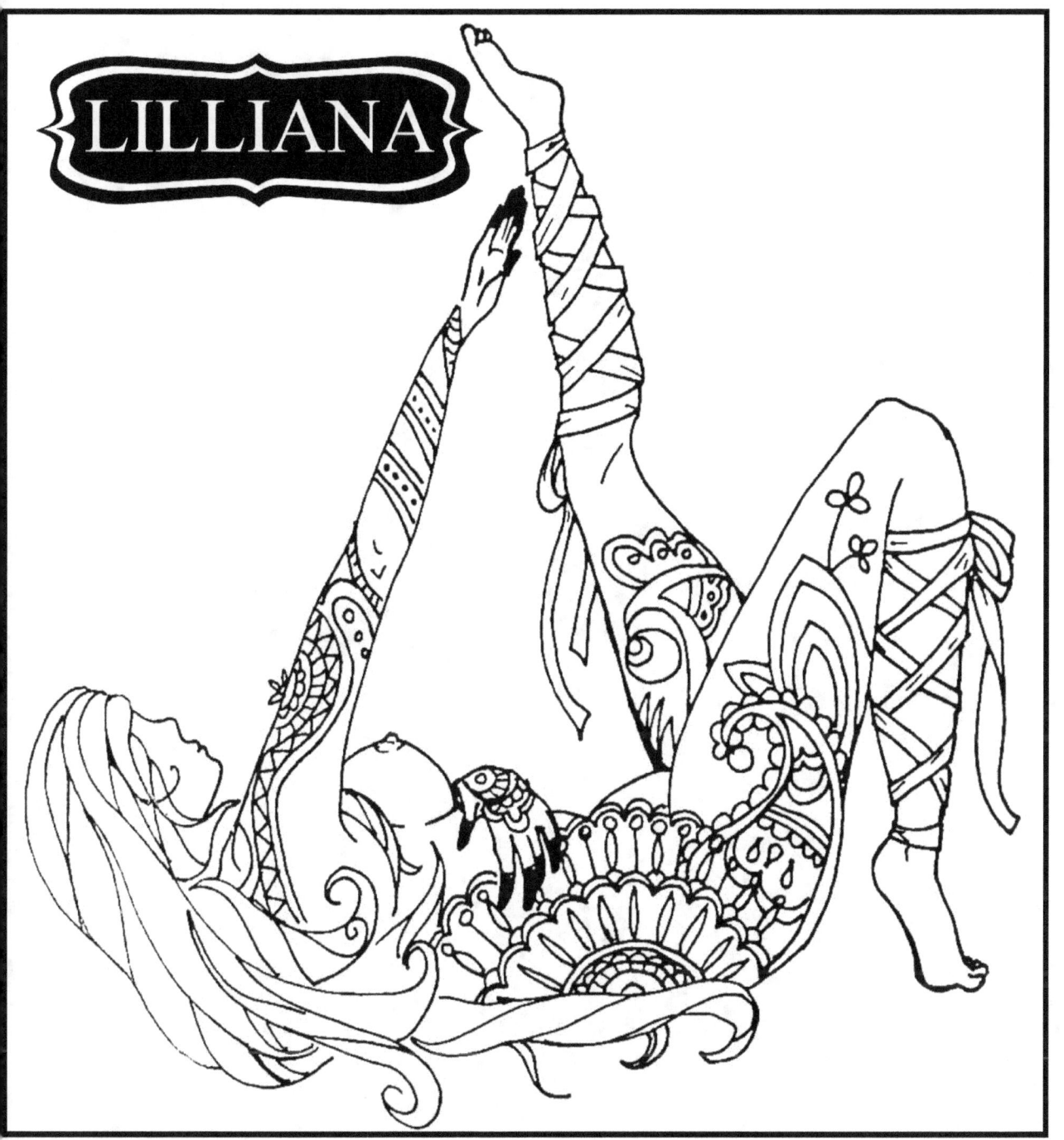

LILLIANA

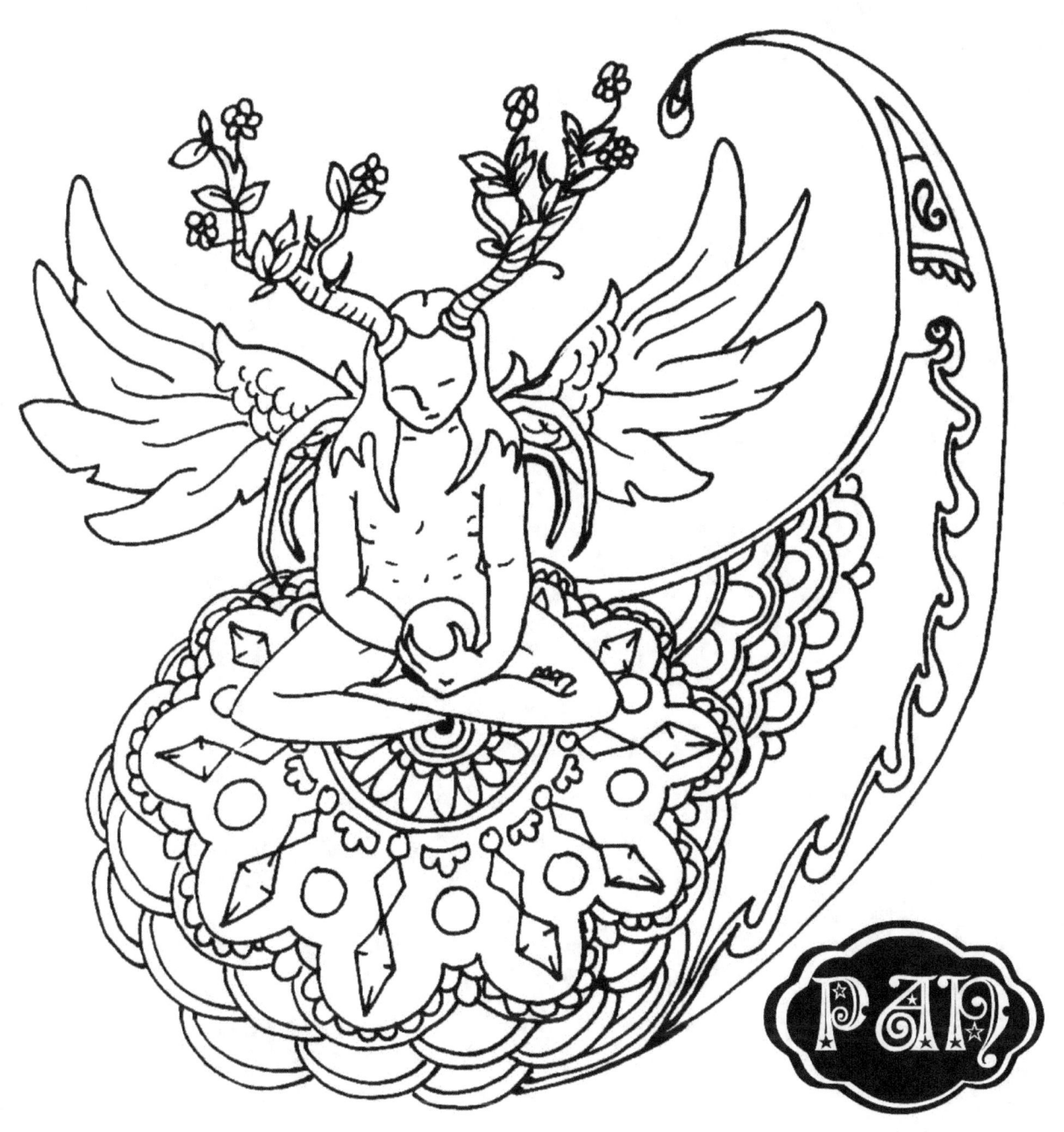

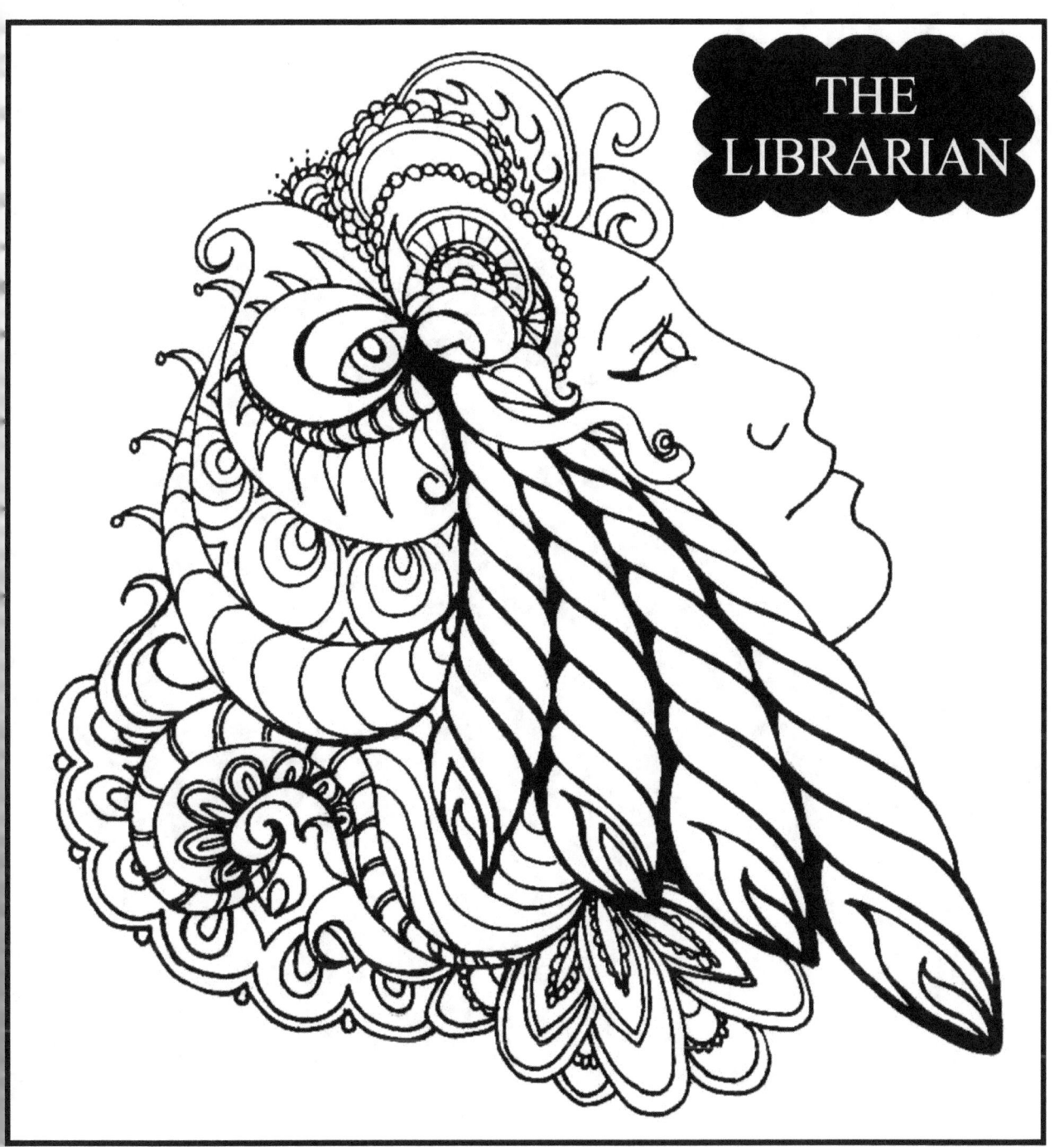

THE LIBRARIAN

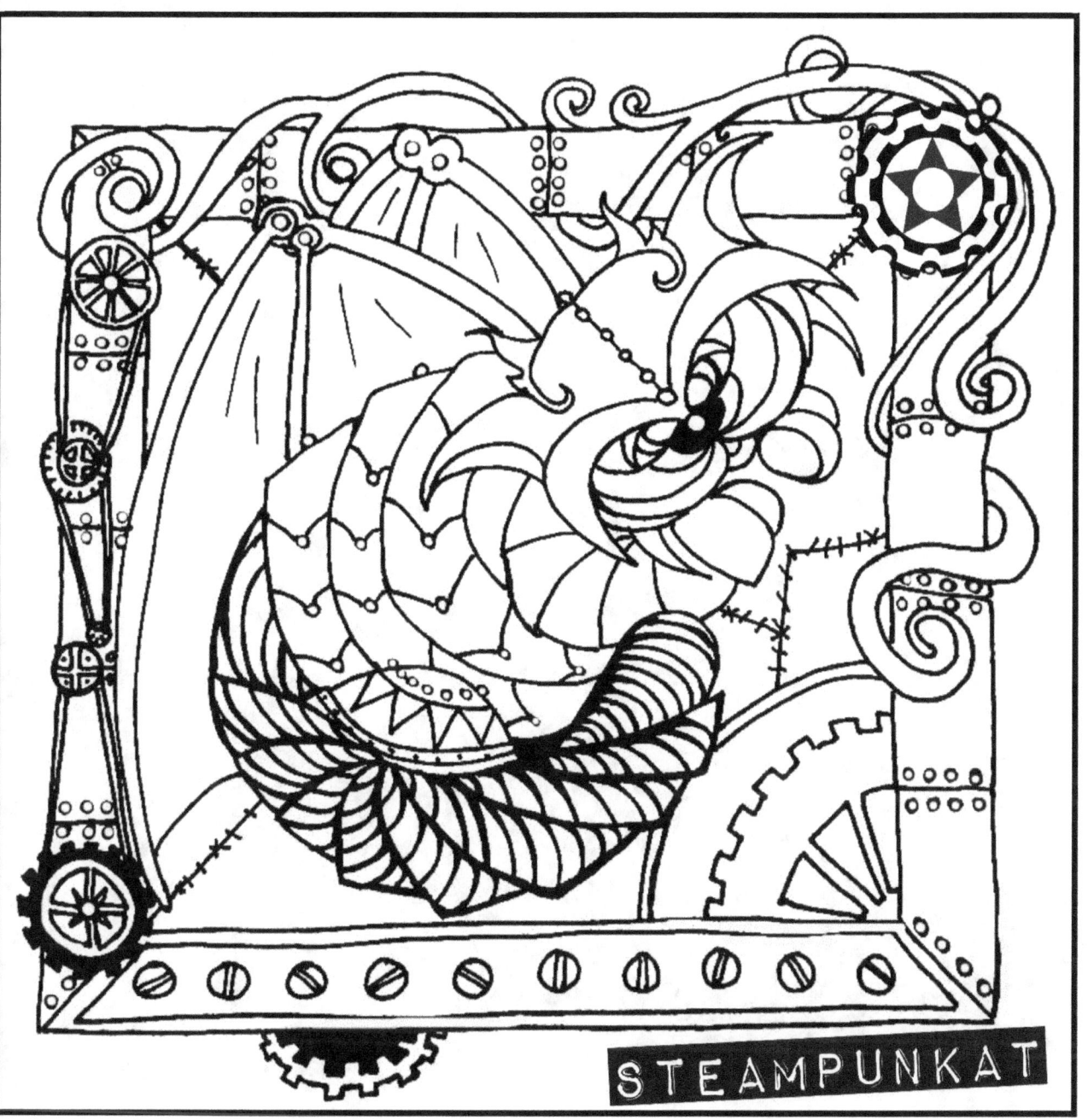

STEAMPUNKAT

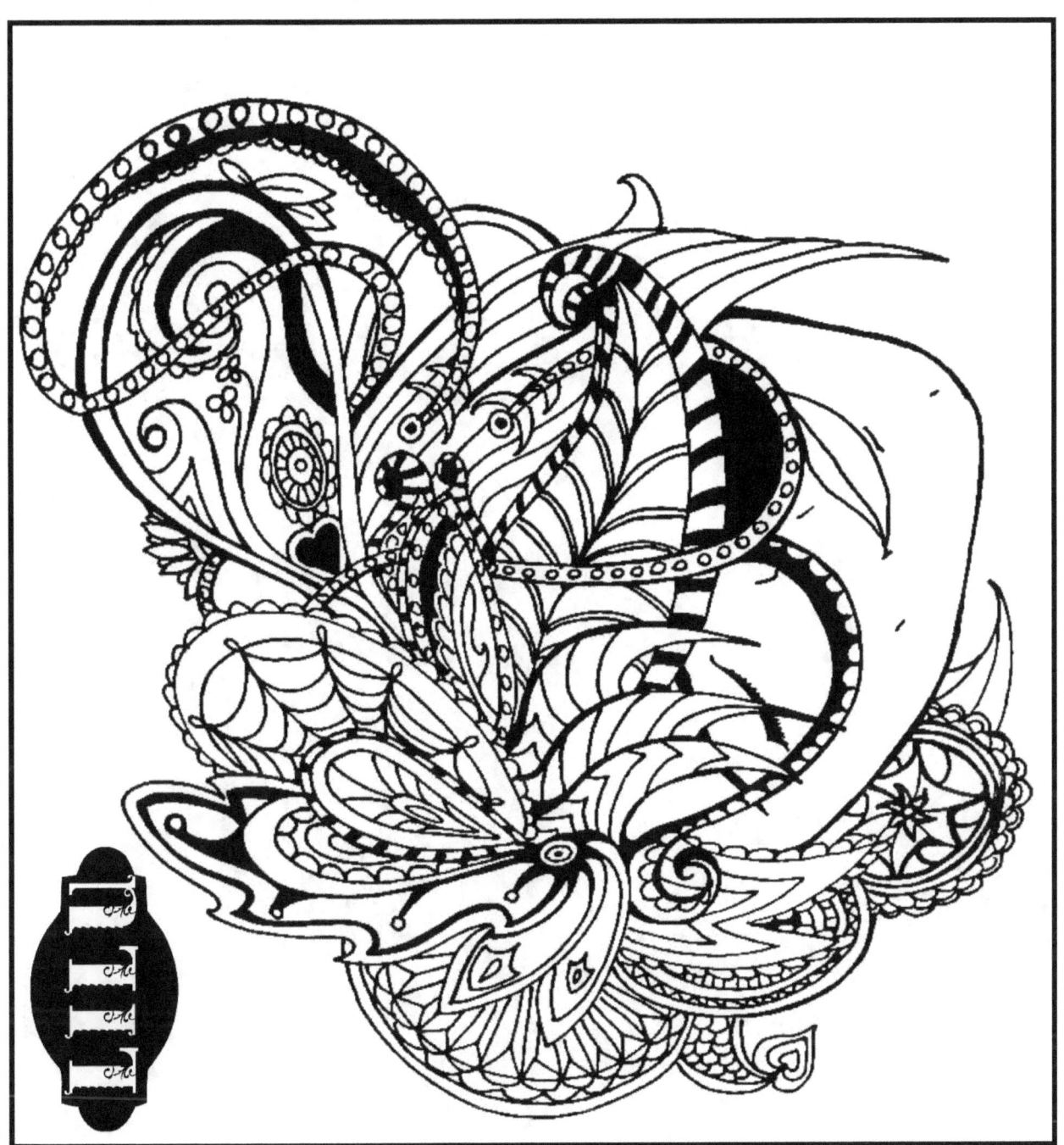

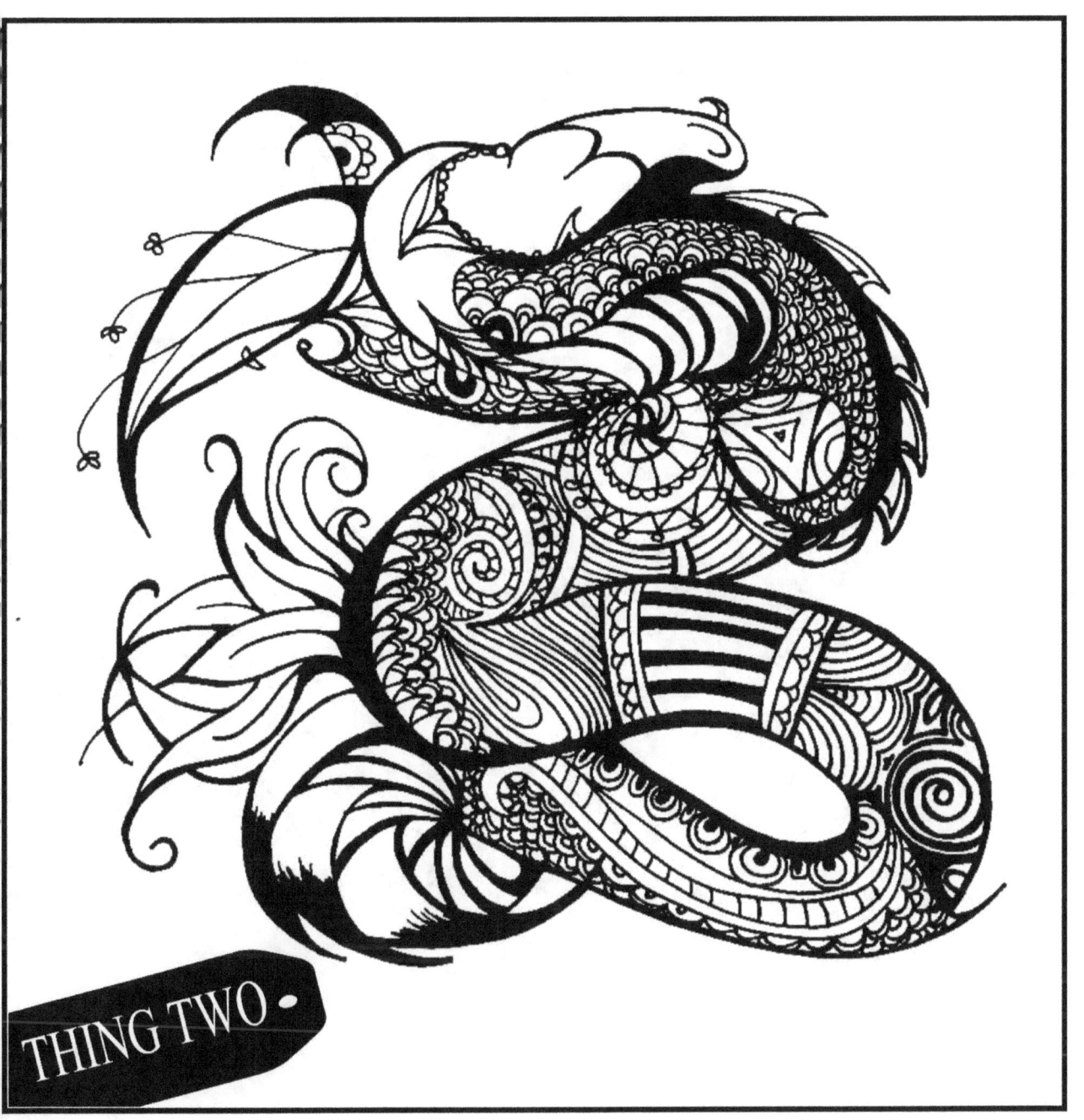

THING TWO

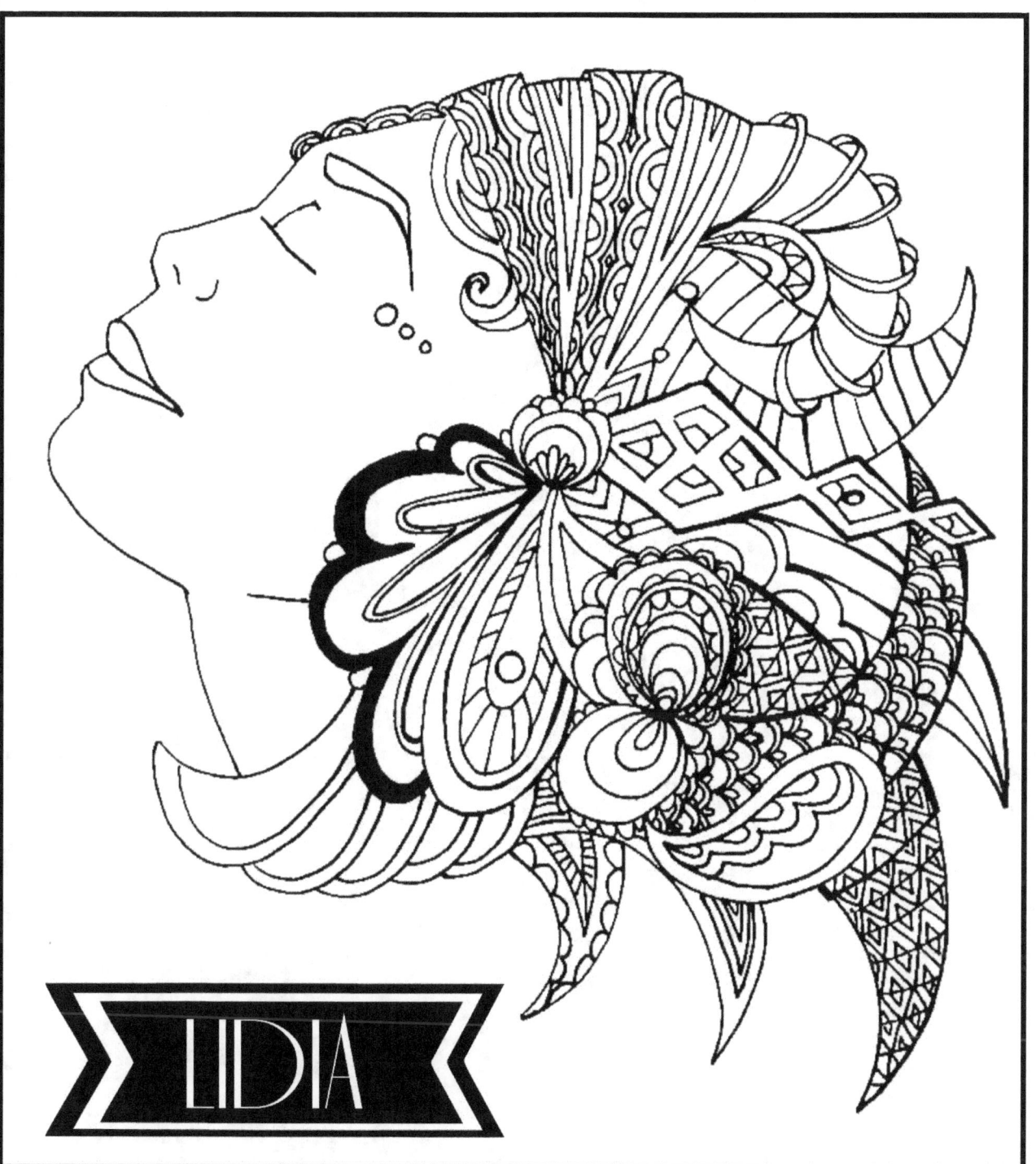

LIDIA

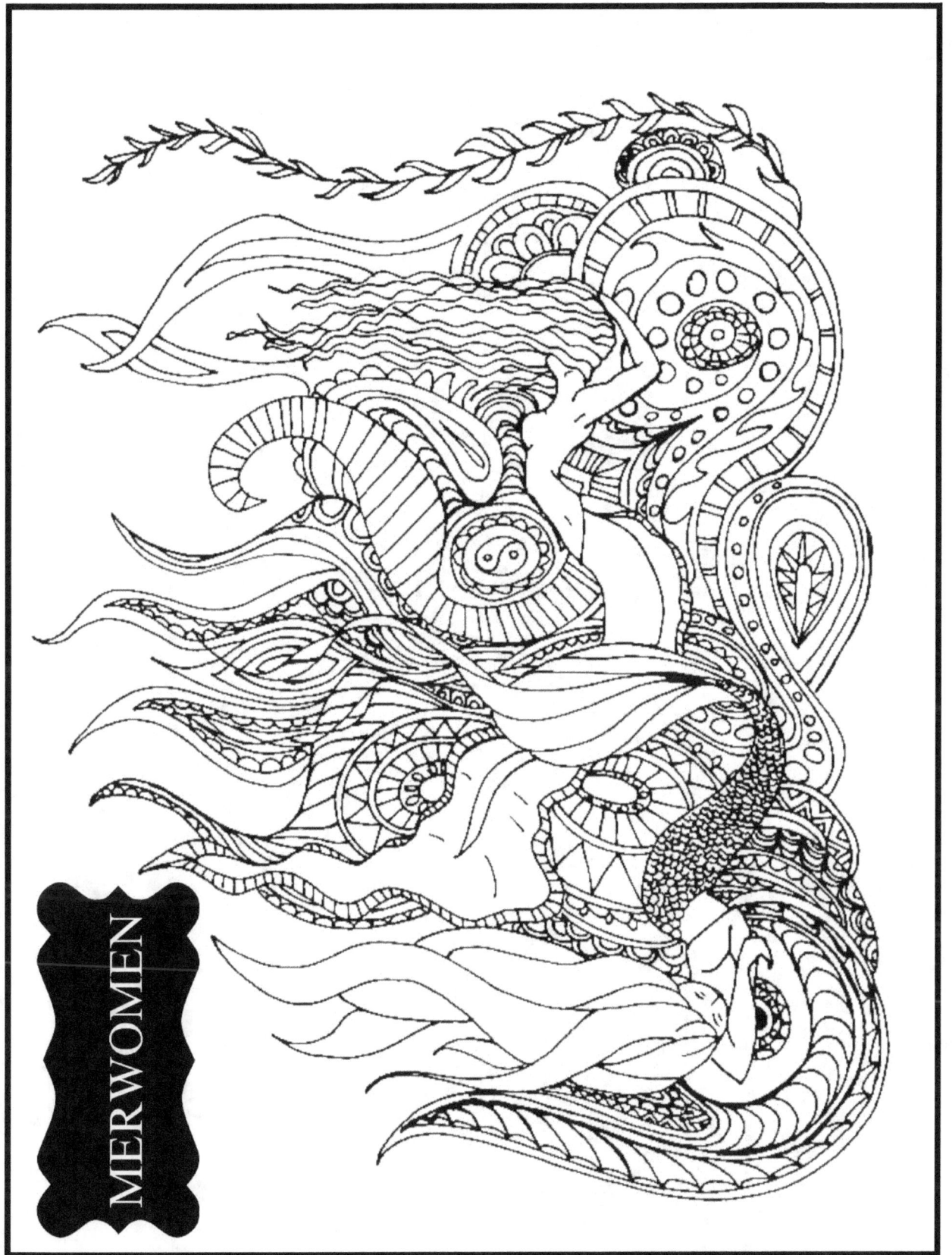

MER WOMEN

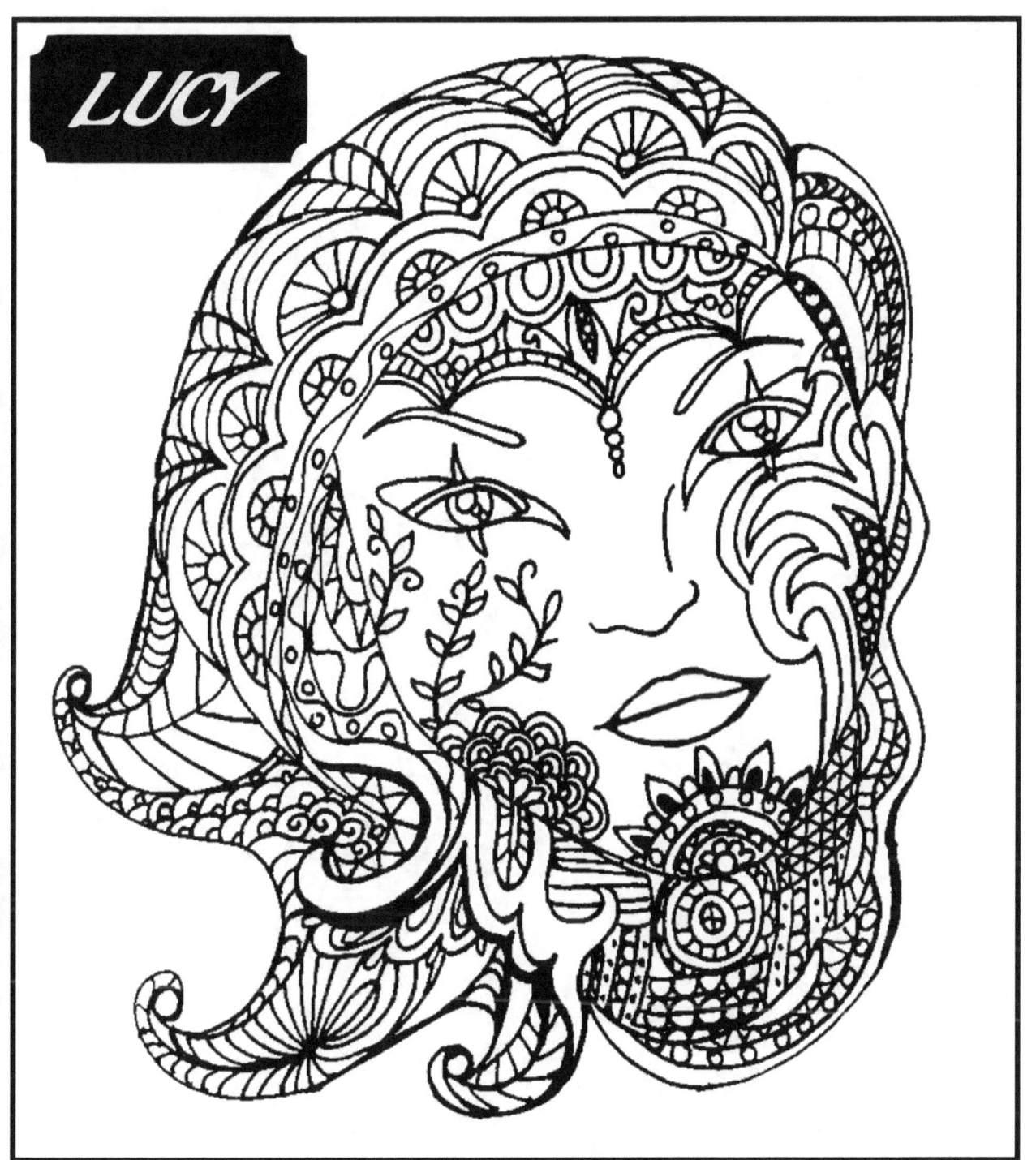

LUCY

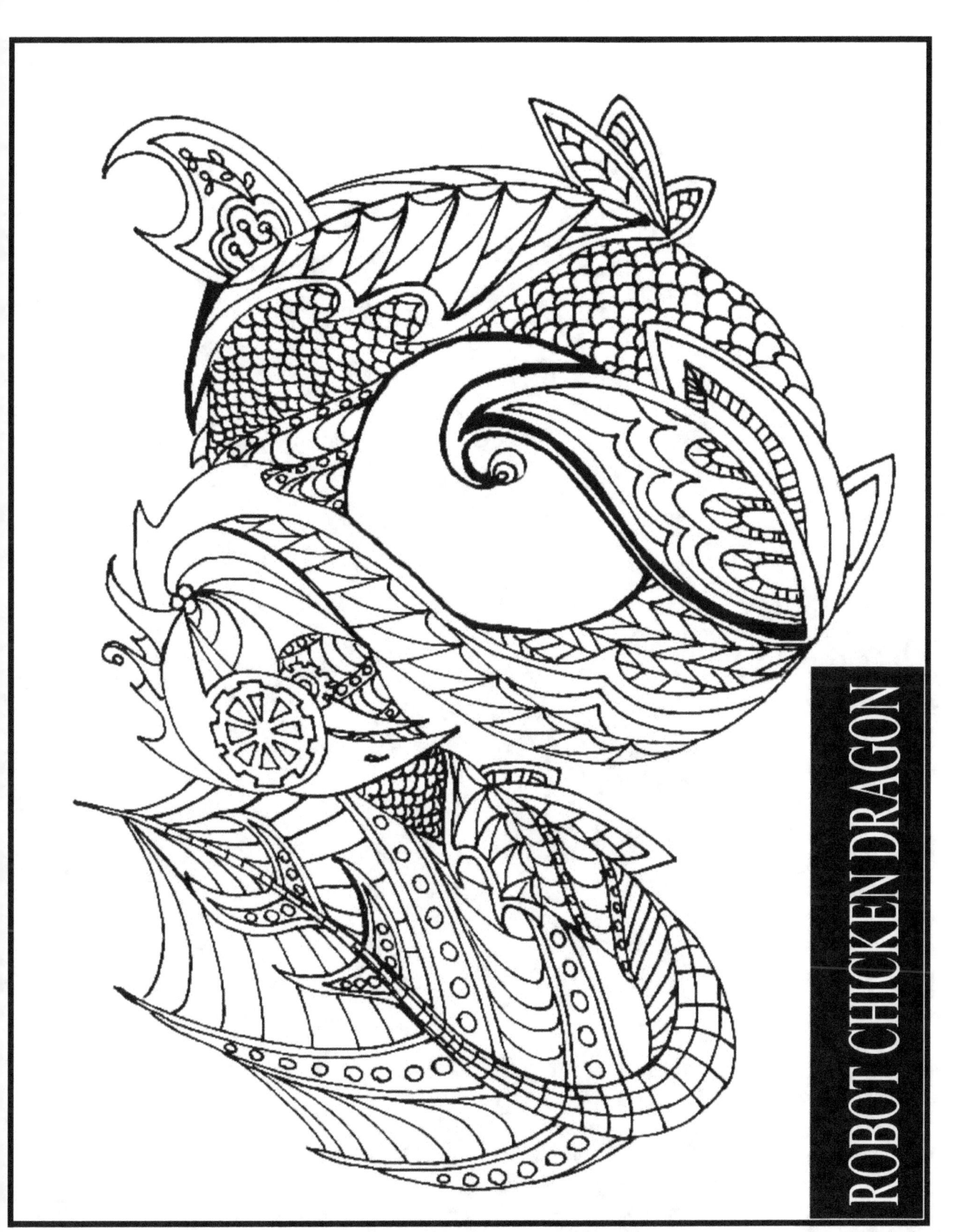

ROBOT CHICKEN DRAGON

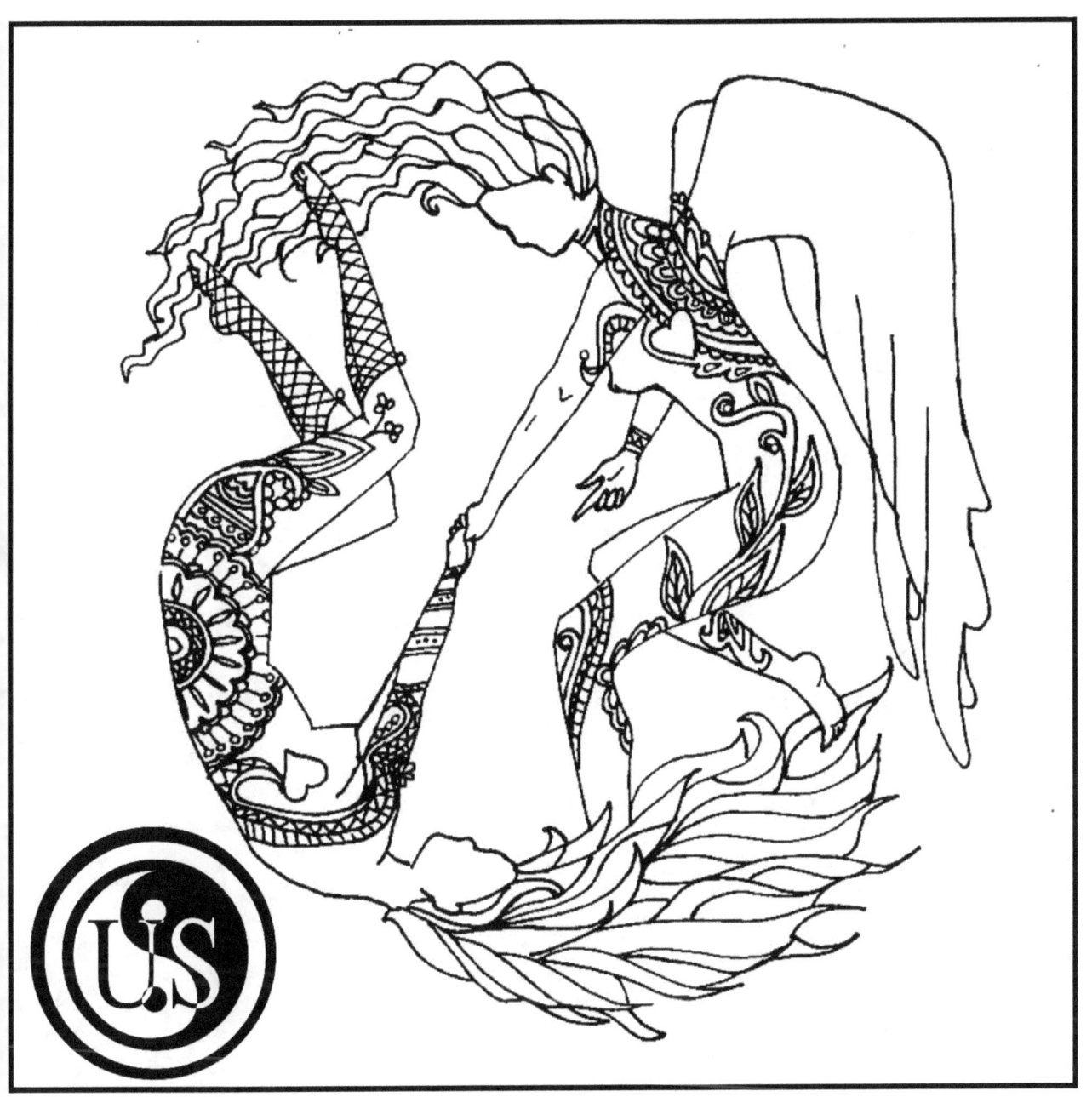

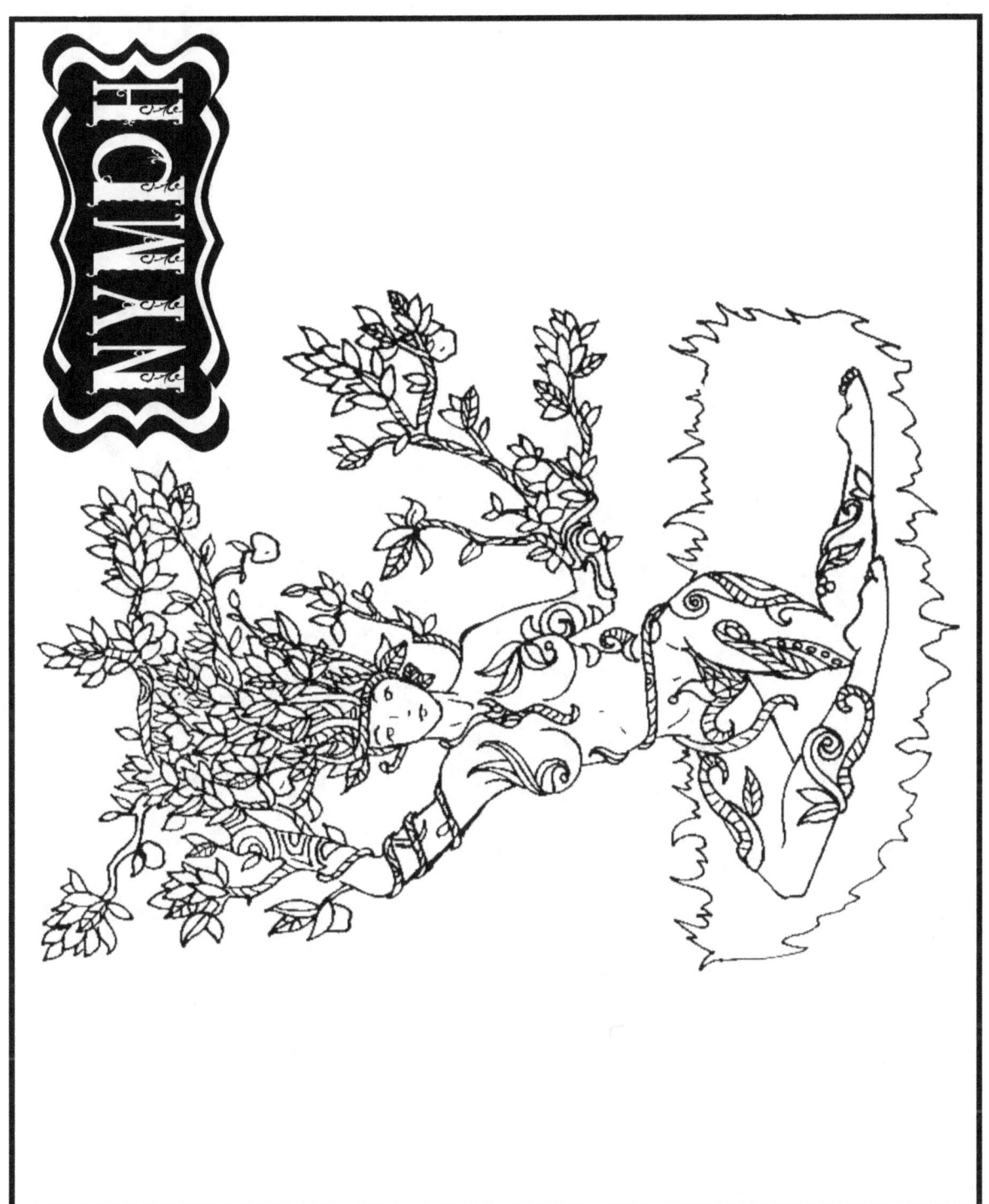

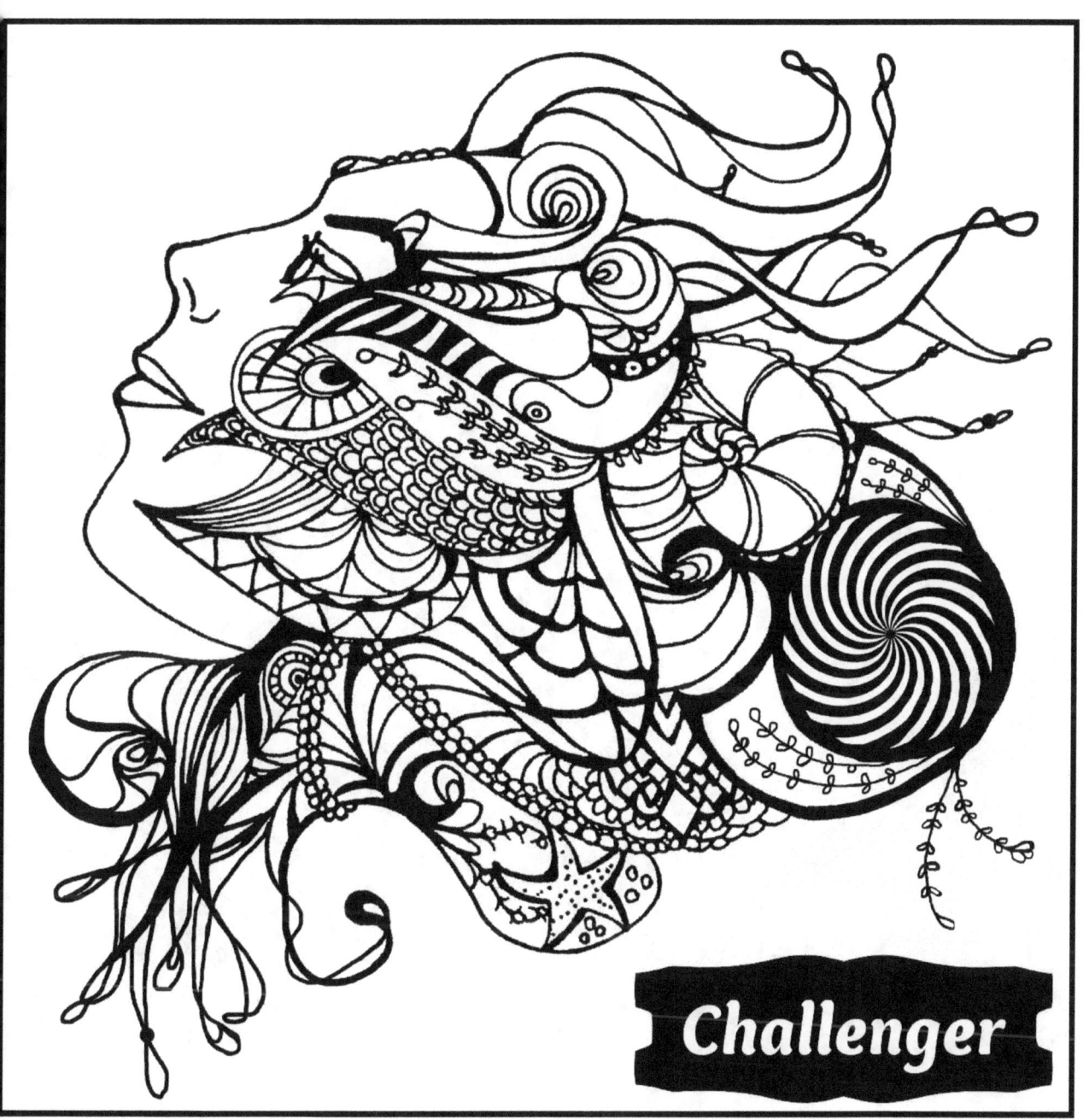

Challenger

Diana Graves Published Works:

THE RAINA KIRKLAND SERIES

Fatal Retribution

Mortal Sentry

Grave Omen

Deadly Encounters

Toxic Warrior

NOVELLAS

The Artist

The Librarian

The Zombie Book

COLORING BOOKS

Dark Whimsy